A Nest for Spring

By Sally Cowan

Gus, Dad and Gwen stand on a strip of cliff.

Can we get some squid?
Not today!
We must set up a nest for spring!

Gus went for a walk.

But that fluff was a fox!
The fluff was the scruff
of his neck.

Gus sprang up to a branch.
It had a bunch of sprigs.

But Gus felt a pinch!

"Scram!" said a thrush.
"That is **my** nest for spring!"

I will just scrap that plan and get some lunch!

Back at home,
the nest was all set
for spring.

"I did not help," said Gus,
with a shrug.
"But I got us lunch!"

CHECKING FOR MEANING

1. What did Gus want to do at the start of the story? *(Literal)*
2. What did he do at the end of the story? *(Literal)*
3. Why do you think Gus wanted to help build the nest? *(Inferential)*

EXTENDING VOCABULARY

strand	What is a *strand*? What does a strand look and feel like? Where might you find a strand?
scruff	In the story, what part of the fox was the scruff? Where is the scruff on a person?
crunch	Say the word *crunch* slowly. What does it mean? *Crunch* is an onomatopoeia, which is a word that sounds like its meaning. Can you think of any other onomatopoeias?

MOVING BEYOND THE TEXT

1. A nest is one type of animal home. Think about where other animals, such as foxes or spiders, live. What other animal homes do you know?
2. Why do you think many birds lay their eggs in a nest? What other animals make nests?
3. What other animals lay eggs? Do mammals lay eggs?
4. Gus saw a fox and thrush on his seaside walk. What might you see if you went for a stroll by the sea?

SPEED SOUNDS

scr	str	spr	nch	squ
shr	thr			

PRACTICE WORDS